I0799291

Inside Public Works

UNDERSTANDING GOVERNMENT

Sonja Reyes

CiViCS FOR THE REAL WORLD™

Rosen Classroom™

Keeping a community looking nice is hard work. Just ask the people in the Public Works Department!

Public works are special projects that are good for the community. The government makes them happen.

Garbage pickup is part of the Public Works Department. It helps keep communities clean.

Sanitation workers drive big trucks around town. They pick up people's garbage and take it away.

Other big trucks collect cans and bottles. These items are recycled or made into new items!

Do you live in a place where it snows a lot? Snowplows are part of the Public Works Department.

Snowplows clear the streets. This makes it safer for people to drive their cars.

The Public Works Department builds bridges. It also fixes roads and broken pipes.

Do you know who keeps parks looking nice? The Public Works Department!

They cut the grass and plant trees and flowers. The Public Works Department makes communities better!

WORDS TO KNOW

bottle

garbage

pipe

snowplow